DEAR NEIGHBOR!

DEAR NEIGHBOR!

Jennifer Miller, Michele J. Wolff,
and Linda Marr

**Andrews McMeel
Publishing**

Kansas City

Dear Neighbor!

Copyright © 2004 by Jennifer Miller, Michele J. Wolff, and Linda Marr. All rights reserved. Printed in Canada. No part of this book may be used or reproduced in any manner whatsoever without written permission except in the case of reprints in the context of reviews. For information, write Andrews McMeel Publishing, an Andrews McMeel Universal company, 4520 Main Street, Kansas City, Missouri 64111.

04 05 06 07 08 TNS 10 9 8 7 6 5 4 3 2 1

ISBN: 0-7407-4638-3

Library of Congress Control Number: 2004101472

Book design by Holly Camerlinck

Dear Neighbor!

Dear new neighbor,

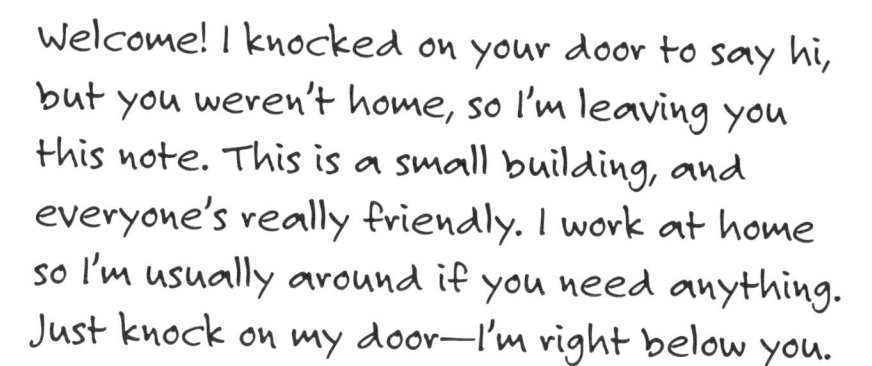

Welcome! I knocked on your door to say hi, but you weren't home, so I'm leaving you this note. This is a small building, and everyone's really friendly. I work at home so I'm usually around if you need anything. Just knock on my door—I'm right below you.

Your neighbor in 103

Dear neighbor,
Got your note. No problem. I'm happy to sign for your package, I'll be here anyway.

Hope to meet you soon!

Dear neighbor,

Glad you got your package. I don't know if you noticed on the receipt that it was sent COD, which I was happy to pay for. So you can just leave a check for $42.50 in my mailbox, although of course I still look forward to meeting you.

Dear neighbor,

Just wanted to make sure you know my mailbox is 103, since it's been a couple days. We don't want old Mr. Taylor in 104 off to Hawaii with my $42.50! (ha, ha) Okay, so just drop it off anytime.

Thanks!

Dear neighbor,

Of course I realize that you didn't authorize me to pay the COD.
I was just trying to do you a favor.

P.S. But even if it is half my fault, shouldn't I at least get $21.25?

Dear neighbor,

Thanks for the See's Candies and your note explaining their approximate value of $23.00. I'd be happy to refund you the $1.75, if the nut clusters and caramels weren't missing. So let's call it even.

Dear neighbor,
Just so you know, when you water your plants, it leaks down to my patio. I think it's because you leave the hose on and go inside for long periods of time.

Thanks.

Dear neighbor,

Maybe you didn't get my note the other day, but anyway I was at the garden store yesterday and saw this watering can (on sale!), and thought it might help.

Enjoy!

Dear neighbor,

I thought I saw the watering can I bought you in the dumpster. Sorry you didn't find it useful, but you shouldn't feel bad about returning it to me. I could've taken it back to the store. (I lied, it wasn't on sale.)

Dear neighbor,

Sorry to keep leaving notes, but when I knocked on your door last night I think you had the music up so loud that you didn't hear me. Which kind of brings me to the point of the note. You're probably not aware that I can hear you above me, and the bass on your stereo actually makes my apartment shake a little (these old buildings!). So if you don't mind, after 11 pm, if you could keep the volume down just a little?

     Thanks, neighbor!

P.S. I waved to you in the parking lot yesterday, but you must not have seen me. Hopefully we can meet someday.

Dear neighbor,

Of course you have a right to listen to music, but others have a right not to hear it after midnight. Maybe late at night you could wear headphones?

Dear neighbor,

Yes, by "others" I did actually mean me. So since I'm the one bothered by this, I did go ahead and buy you some headphones. Hope this is a good compromise.

Dear neighbor,

I got your note. Sorry these were such "shitty" headphones. I appreciate you returning them this time. Unfortunately I can't take them back to the store now because they're broken.

Dear neighbor,

I just wanted to point out that the white parallel lines mark the delineation of your parking space and mine. I guess that's not something you would know, being new to the building. Please try to park more in your own space, so that we can equally enjoy the covered parking.

Dear neighbor,

No, of course it's not your fault that our parking spaces are compact, and there is not a lot of room to open doors. Again, there's a lot more room when your car is parked BETWEEN those two parallel white lines I mentioned before. Also, I'm sure it was an accident, but you did ding my car. I'm not going to ask you to pay (although I could), but please try to be more careful in the future.

Thank you.

Dear neighbor,

Congratulations on your new dog. He's really cute. Even though dogs are technically not allowed in the building, I won't say anything because I'm an animal lover too and it's great you're giving him a good home. A lot of people in apartments won't adopt the really large dogs.

Dear neighbor,

Just wanted you to know I had to take a taxi to a meeting this morning. It turned out that when I went to get my car, your girlfriend's car was blocking mine. I knocked on your door, but no one answered. Please let her know that guest parking is around the other side. Or maybe she could park in front of <u>your</u> car?

Dear neighbor,

I understand that it would be inconvenient for you to have to move two cars in the morning in order to get yours out. And yes, I did tell you I worked at home, but I do occasionally leave my house. That's why I have a car.

Dear neighbor,

You're gone all day so I'm not sure you're aware of this. But your dog can't handle being tied up on your balcony eight hours a day. I know this because he barks and howls constantly. Maybe he could go to doggy day care?

Dear neighbor,
Thank you for telling me where I can go, but I'm not sure that hell would be any more torturous than having to listen to a dog barking eight hours a day followed by the insanely loud bass pounding pounding pounding over my head all night long! Enclosed please find a copy of our local noise ordinance.

Dear neighbor,

Thank you for returning the copy of the ordinance. I don't think it was necessary to call me a bitter, dried-up old spinster. I'm 29. And it would be easier to find a boyfriend if I could bring him back to my apartment.

Dear neighbor,

The couch you left in the courtyard is blocking my front entrance. I moved it aside so I could get into my apartment, but you need to please get rid of it.

Dear neighbor,

No, I don't think the courtyard "needed a couch." Perhaps if it were a <u>new</u> couch, or at least one that still had cushions. Thank you for your consideration.

Dear neighbor,

I noticed a large volume of trash in the stairwell this morning, coinciding with the party that you had last night. Which brings me to my next point. Our balconies are rather small, and are not meant to hold 30-40 people. And had you read the noise ordinance, you would know that a loud party that late at night is a violation.

Dear neighbor,

I appreciate that you feel that you invited me to the party. Perhaps if you want me to attend in the future, you can send a more formal invitation, instead of leaning over the balcony and screaming "if you don't like it come up here and do something about it, bitch."

Dear neighbor,

Why don't we make a deal? I will agree to keep my windows and doors closed (which will not be easy since, as you know, we have no air-conditioning in this building). In return, perhaps you can try, just a little, to keep the noise down? Thank you.

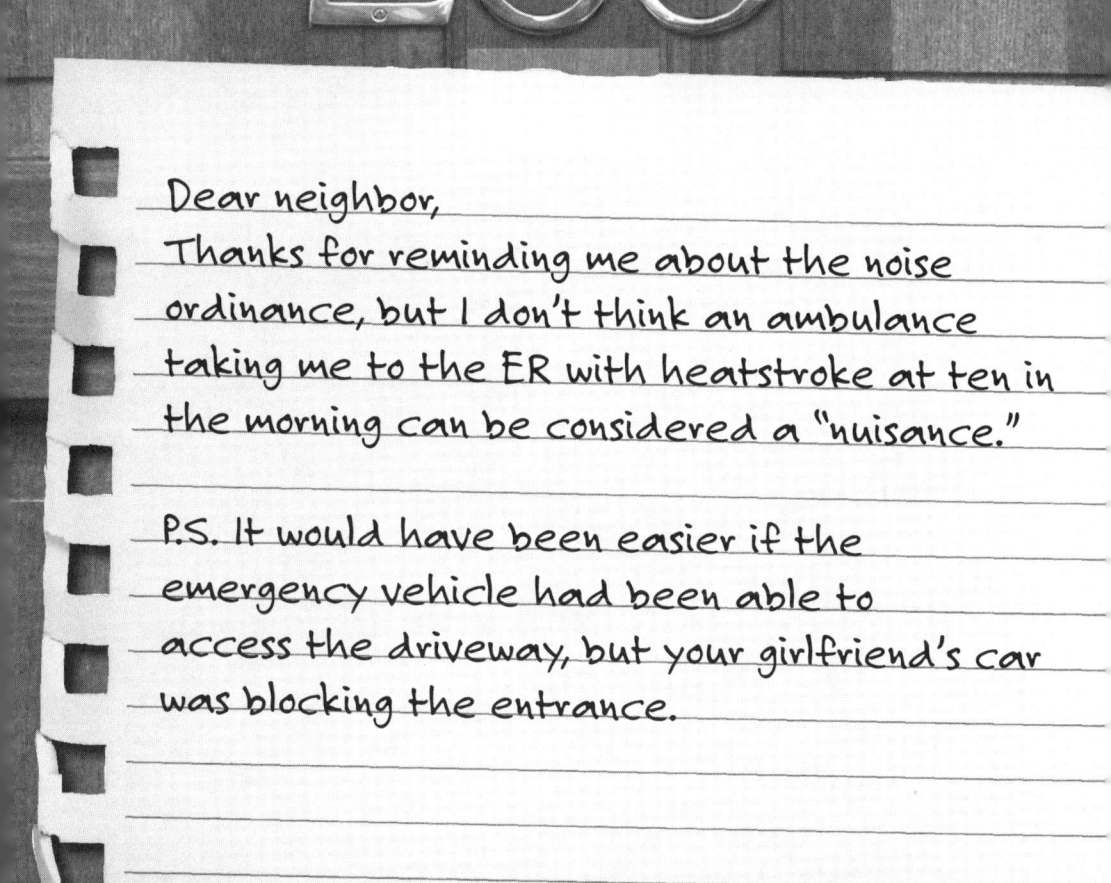

Dear neighbor,

Thanks for reminding me about the noise ordinance, but I don't think an ambulance taking me to the ER with heatstroke at ten in the morning can be considered a "nuisance."

P.S. It would have been easier if the emergency vehicle had been able to access the driveway, but your girlfriend's car was blocking the entrance.

Dear neighbor,
Just wondered if you were ever planning to move the couch? It is now covered in bird shit. And something's been gnawing on it. Rats?

Dear neighbor, I have the Sunday paper delivered as a matter of convenience. Lately I have been receiving it on Tuesday, with many sections missing. I think I should be able to enjoy the whole paper, including lifestyle, TV guide, and particularly sports.

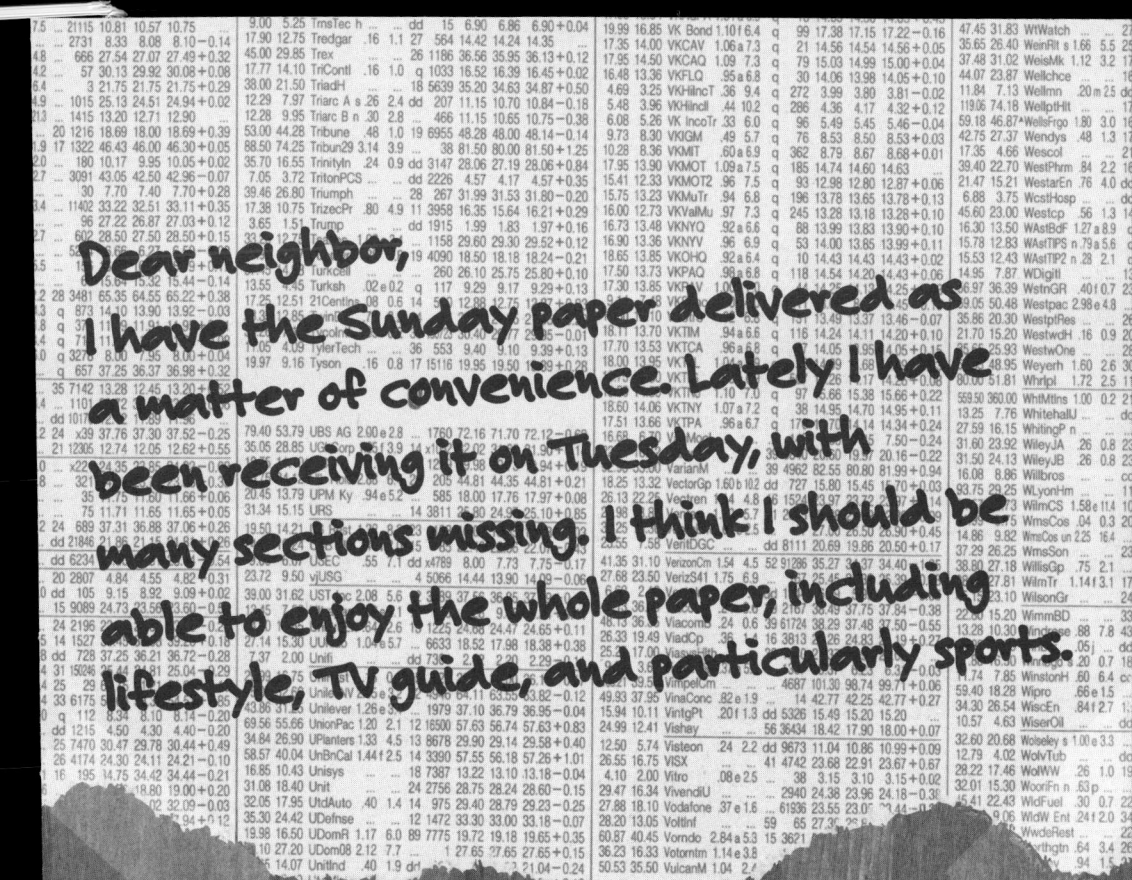

Dear neighbor,

No, I am not a lesbian. And while I appreciate that I am "lucky I got a paper at all," I would still prefer one that is complete.

Dear neighbor,
I appreciate that I got a full paper today (and it's only Monday!). However, I do not believe the publisher circled that article on frigidity and menopause. I am 29.

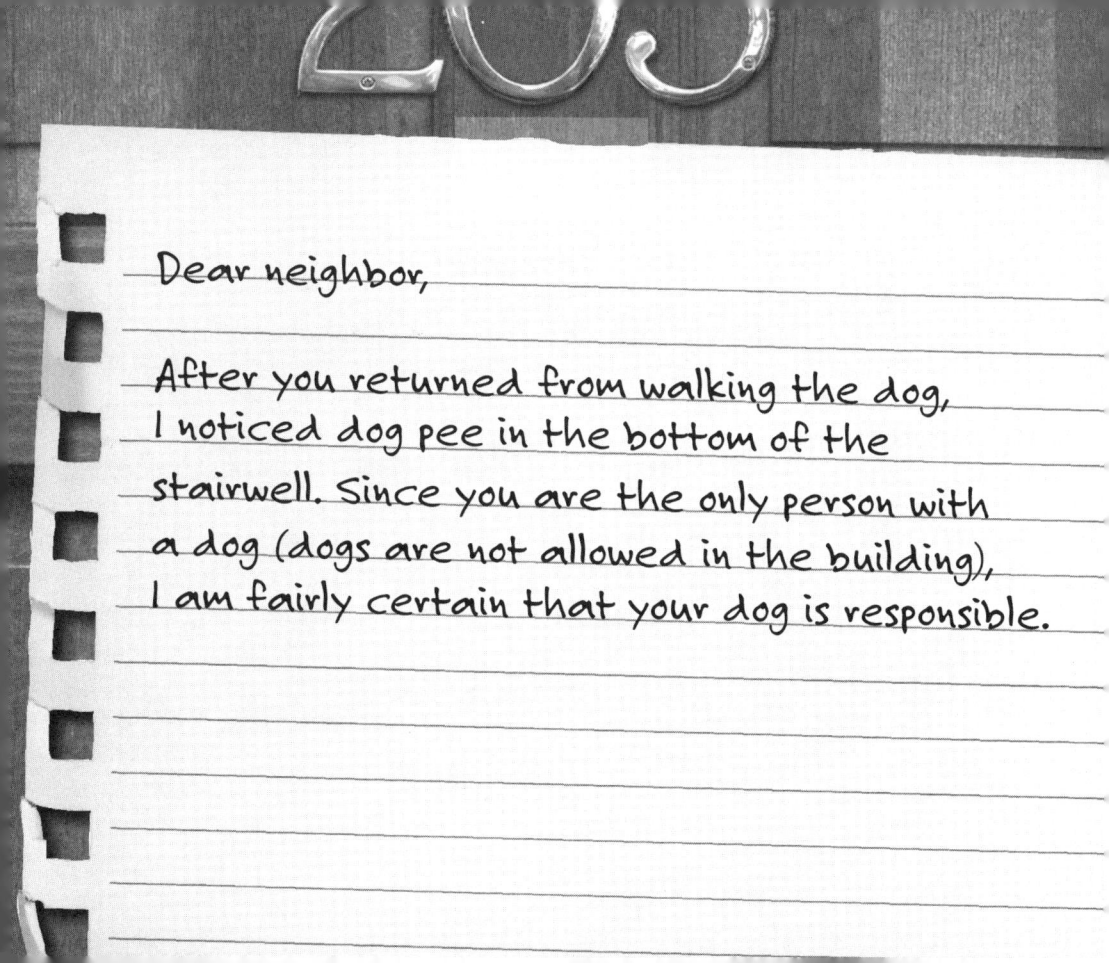

Dear neighbor,

After you returned from walking the dog, I noticed dog pee in the bottom of the stairwell. Since you are the only person with a dog (dogs are not allowed in the building), I am fairly certain that your dog is responsible.

Dear neighbor,

You bring up an interesting point. I did jump to conclusions that it was dog pee. I have since had the pee analyzed. It is not dog pee, and it matches the pee left in front of my door.

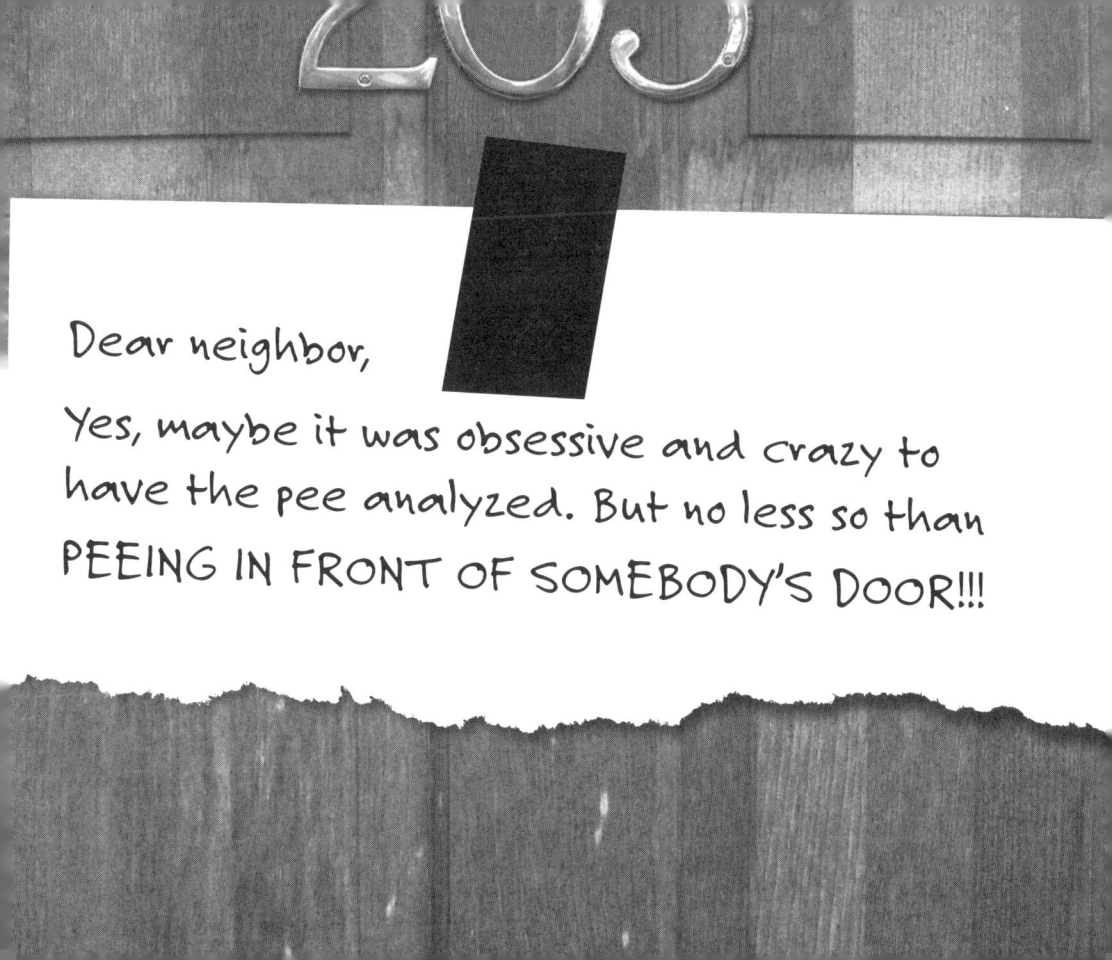

Dear neighbor,

Yes, maybe it was obsessive and crazy to have the pee analyzed. But no less so than PEEING IN FRONT OF SOMEBODY'S DOOR!!!

Dear neighbor,

I have contacted our landlord and told him everything. If he spoke English you'd be in some big trouble right now.

DEAR NEIGHBOR,
IS IT ME?! IS IT ME?! I'VE ALWAYS GOTTEN ALONG SO WELL WITH MY NEIGHBORS!

Dear neighbor,

No, I did not "steal" your couch. Besides the aforementioned rats and bird shit, after four weeks in the rain it began to mildew and smell, so I paid to have it hauled away.

YOU'RE WELCOME.

Dear neighbor,

Yes, I _am_ very proud of my "priss-ass" vocabulary. In the future I will try to use smaller words than "aforementioned." By the way, it means "mentioned before."

Dear neighbor,

I understand you have an old battery, but revving your car for 30 minutes every morning outside my window at 6:00 am is starting to get really annoying. I think you need to get a new battery.

P.S. Don't you ever sleep?

Dear neighbor,

When I suggested you get a new battery I was thinking that perhaps you would <u>purchase</u> one. I guess the joke's on me. I am not accusing anyone, but when I went to start my car this morning, I realized my battery was missing. Any thoughts?

Dear neighbor,

It _does_ matter. Again, I _do_ leave the house, and I _do_ need my car, and my car needs a battery! And I do not think "turnabout is fair play" for stealing your beloved couch. It was a piece of shit and I PAID TO HAVE IT TAKEN AWAY!

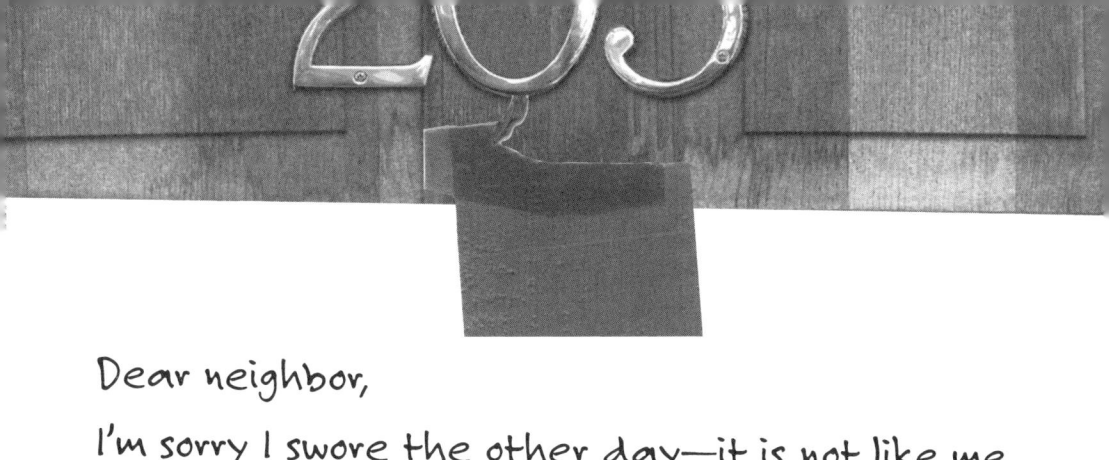

Dear neighbor,

I'm sorry I swore the other day—it is not like me.

However, I do not think that makes me castrating.

It's just the lack of sleep.

Dear neighbor,

Fine, call the police about your stupid "stolen" couch. When they arrive, perhaps I can have them analyze the pee on my front door for DRUGS.

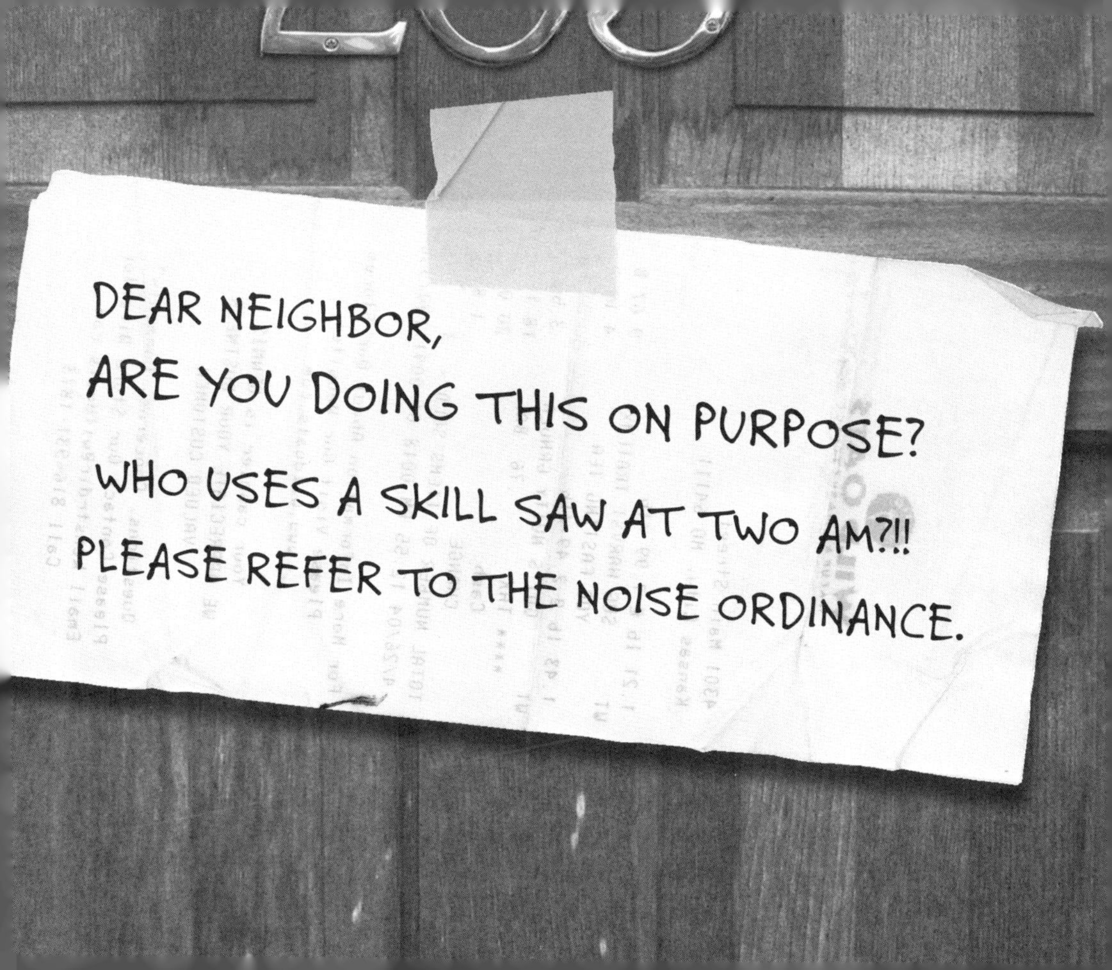
DEAR NEIGHBOR,
ARE YOU DOING THIS ON PURPOSE?
WHO USES A SKILL SAW AT TWO AM?!!
PLEASE REFER TO THE NOISE ORDINANCE.

Dear neighbor,

It's faulty logic that "if you pay rent, you can do whatever the hell you want."

DO NOT USE CONSTRUCTION EQUIPMENT IN THE MIDDLE OF THE NIGHT!!!

Dear neighbor,
Yes, I really did call the police. You didn't think I had it in me, did you? You don't know what I'm going to do next. Although in the future I will take into consideration that you own a police scanner and will "always be one step ahead of me."

Dear neighbor,

As per your comment that I am the "only bitch complaining"—enclosed please find signatures from several other tenants.

Dear neighbor,

No, I am not trying to turn everyone against you.

Dear neighbor,

No, I am not obsessed with you, and I do not appreciate you telling everyone in the building that I am. I am only obsessed with a good night's sleep. Which brings me to tomorrow. I have a very important job interview early in the morning. If you can stop making noise for ONE NIGHT, I can get to the interview, get a better job, leave this building, and stop writing these letters!

Dear neighbor,

After getting to bed around 3:00 am, (again, coincidentally right around the time your nightly party ended), I overslept right through my job interview. Which means I did not get the job, I will never save any money, I will never have enough to get out of here! Ever, ever, EVER!

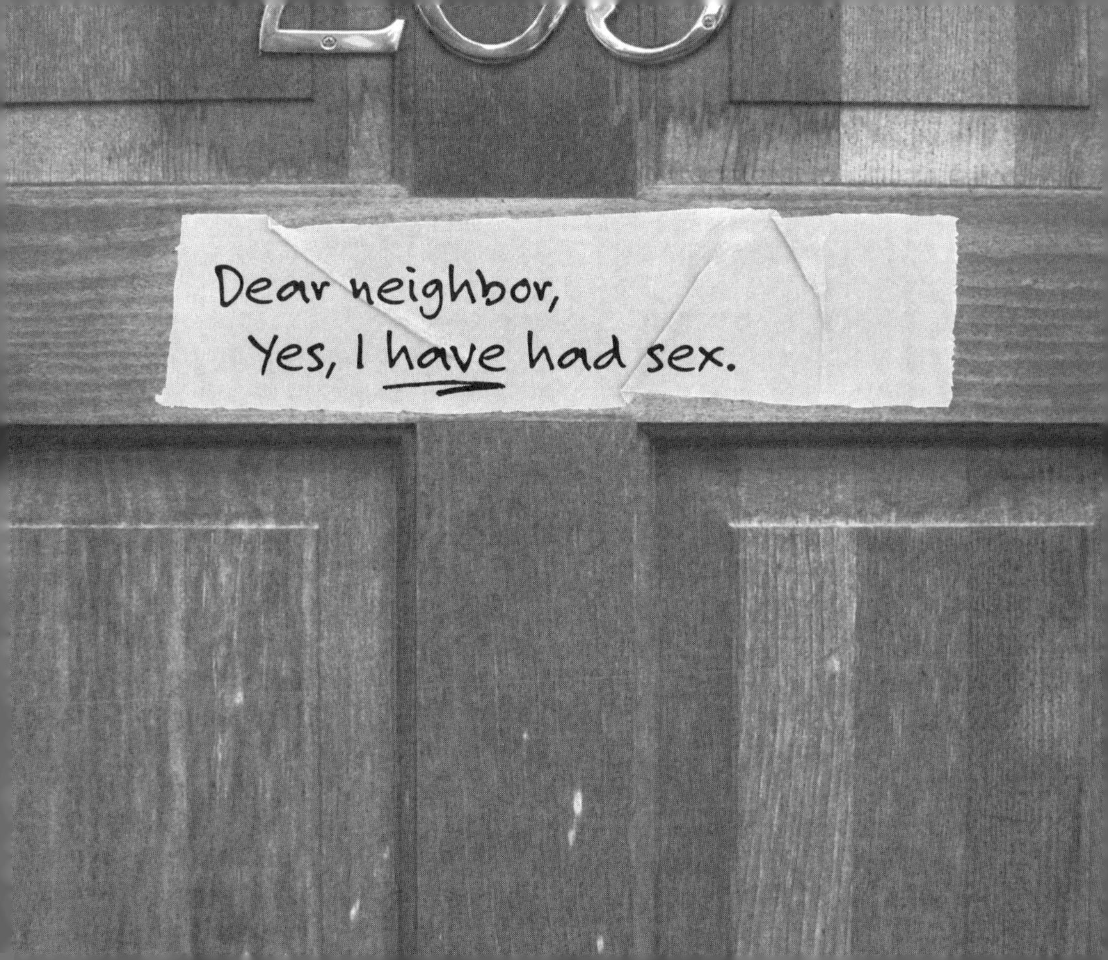
Dear neighbor,
Yes, I have had sex.

Dear neighbor,
Yes, with men.

DEAR NEIGHBOR,
UNBELIEVABLE! MY LITTLE NIECE CAN'T EVEN SELL GIRL SCOUT COOKIES IN MY OWN BUILDING! COMMENTING ON HER GETTING "BOOBIES" AT AN EARLY AGE IS INAPPROPRIATE AND <u>DISGUSTING</u> COMING FROM A GROWN MAN.

P.S. "PUT IT ON YOUR AUNT'S TAB" IS NOT REALLY A SALE. ENJOY YOUR THIN MINTS, FUCKWAD.

Dear neighbor,

I do not appreciate you leaving Polaroids of your naked ass on my car.

Dear neighbor,

~~[scribbled out]~~

No, I do not know for sure that it's <u>your</u> ass, but it looks suspiciously like the one that was hanging over your balcony the other night, with the entreaties to "kiss this, bitch."

FIRST CLASS MAIL
U.S. POSTAGE PAID
ABF

Dear neighbor,

Look, I've asked nicely, I've been patient, I've tried to compromise. What can I possibly do to get you to show me a modicum of consideration?

Dear neighbor,
Thanks for your clever suggestion.
But if I am going to do anything that involves me getting on my hands and knees, it will be to pray to God for

A NEW NEIGHBOR THAT ISN'T

A SELF-ABSORBED SHITHEAD!!!!

DEAR NEIGHBOR,

NO, I AM NOT ON MY PERIOD. AND YES, I STILL GET ONE. I'M 29, YOU PRICK!

Dear neighbor,

I have had it with you! You've made my life miserable! If you so much as drop a paper clip, I'm calling the cops.

I'M NOT FUCKING KIDDING.

P.S. Just bought a little something called "Scanner Jammer." Who's one step ahead now?

Your move, dickhead!

Dear neighbor,
You think I don't know you scratched that on my car?! You think I'm that stupid?! The C's and T's look exactly like the writing in your notes, which I have **kept** as **evidence**.

THE COPS WILL THINK SO TOO!!!!

Don't threaten me! Don't you dare threaten me! I will destroy you!

DEAR INCONSIDERATE ASSHOLE!

Here is an itemized list of EVERYTHING I HAVE SPENT MONEY ON BECAUSE OF YOU. Just wanted you to know:

- Headphones
- Watering can
- Ear plugs
- Prozac
- Doctor visits (3)
- ER visit (heatstroke)
- Couch removal
- Doormat
- Car ding repair
- Car paint job (scratch removal, etc)
- White noise device
- Taxi fare
- Sleeping pills
- Alcohol
- ER visit (stomach pumping)
- COD charge (partial)
- Gun

LEAVE THIS BUILDING OR YOU WILL DIE!

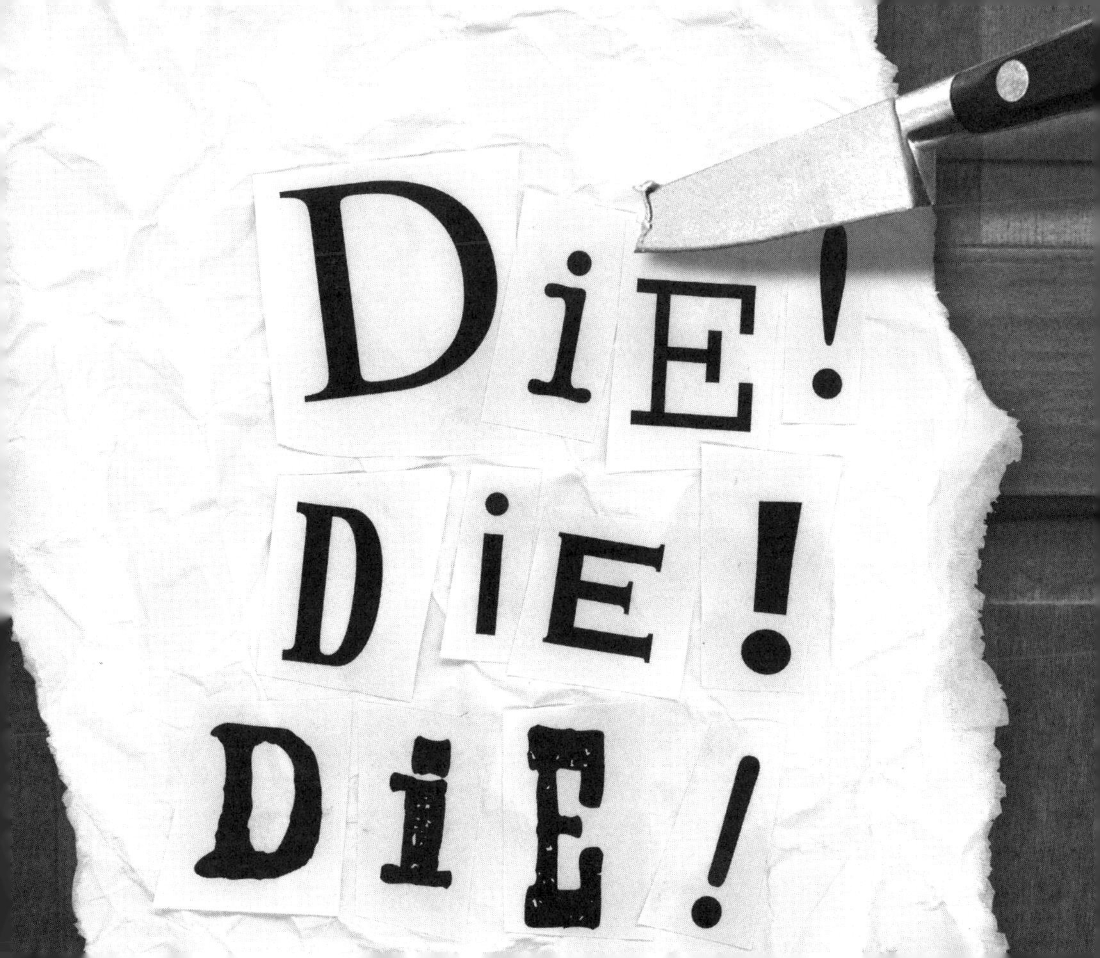
DiE!
DiE!
DiE!

DOESN'T ANYTHING I SAY MAKE A DIFFERENCE?!!!! DON'T YOU LISTEN, DON'T YOU UNDERSTAND?! I KNOW YOU'RE THERE. I CAN HEAR YOU. I CAN HEAR YOU!! EVEN WHEN I'M NOT HERE THE NOISE IS IN MY HEAD! TWENTY-FOUR HOURS A DAY! YOU NEVER GO AWAY! YOU NEVER SHUT UP!!! WHY ARE YOU TORTURING ME? WHY?!! WHY?!! DEAR GOD, PLEASE HELP ME!!

Dear neighbor's mother,

So sorry to hear about your son. He only lived here a short time, but we were in constant contact. I had warned him repeatedly that the balcony wasn't safe and was in danger of collapse. The police said it looked like one of his party guests, in some kind of drunken revelry, and for some unknown motive, might even have loosened the bolts on the railing! Sadly they'll never know who, because there were so very many of them. Your son certainly had a lust for life, and it won't be the same here without him.

Your late son's neighbor in 103